A portion of the
proceeds from each book
will be donated to the
Doernbecher Children's
Hospital Patient Care Fund.
The fund supports patient
care for those unable to pay.
The patient care centers are
dedicated to the most
seriously ill and injured
children.

In loving memory
of my parents.

Books by Janelle Lombard

Menus From The Pacific Northwest - Volume I
Menus From The Pacific Northwest - Volume II
Lite Pacific Northwest Recipes
Main Course Salads For Two From The Pacific Northwest

Printed and bound in the United States of America

Library of Congress Control Number: 2003109950
ISBN 0961552549

Main Course Salads
For Two
From
The Pacific Northwest

by Janelle Lombard

This fourth book in my series of cookbooks—Main Course Salads For Two—features today's popular entrée choice. Lightness and freshness, simple preparation, and great tasting casual meals make this book a must for your cookbook library.

The Pacific Northwest lifestyle values the "quality of life", the love of nature, and the willingness to explore new ideas. Close proximity to the natural rugged beauty of the wilderness provides many forms of recreational activities, resulting in a fast-paced, nutritionally conscious population. The attraction of many people to this area indicates that this way of life is a model for all areas of the country. Health conscious people everywhere are taking deliberate steps to enjoy an active lifestyle, and more healthful weight—enabled by today's trend toward lighter, healthier cooking. These main course salads are a perfect complement to this.

Salads have undergone a dramatic transformation from a simple side dish to "center stage" at lunch and dinner. Their versatility makes them a favorite of chefs; however, the creation of a "serious" salad can be accomplished easily by the novice cook. Natural, local fresh products and exciting combinations of ingredients make these meals interesting.

A cooking revolution has emerged as the number of one and two person households has grown to over 54%. Cooking for one or two is a part of our lives at many stages—newlyweds, single parents, new parents, college students, singles, or shrinking households. With the simple preparation of salads, some requiring no cooking at all, couples can cook together, save the expense of eating out, and eat healthfully. The portions discourage the temptation for "second helpings" and the often discarded leftovers. On the other hand, if you are entertaining, just double the recipe.

The main course salads in this book are fresh, chic, and quick to prepare. In many of the recipes you can substitute the precooked foods readily available in today's markets, saving even more time. To expedite shopping, I have included a "Stocking Your Pantry" list for all of the recipes in the book, so that you have a very short list of fresh ingredients to buy. Just plan your meals for the week and shop once!

Your choices about lifestyle are key, and the "center stage" salad fits, in a positive way, our twenty-first century life. Explore these recipes, be creative by adding new ingredients, and experience the satisfaction and accomplishment of cooking.

Bon Appétit!

Janelle Lombard

Stocking Your Pantry

Having the following staples on hand will simplify your shopping. In the ingredients list for each recipe, items listed by a ✦ should be purchased fresh.

Oils:
extra virgin olive oil
salad oil
peanut oil
canola oil
sesame oil
hot chili oil

Vinegars:
white wine vinegar
white vinegar
rice wine vinegar
balsamic vinegar
tarragon vinegar
dry sherry
red wine vinegar

Grains and Pasta:
long grain white rice
bow tie pasta
farfalle pasta
capellini pasta
penne pasta
orecchiette pasta
cornstarch
flour
bisquick

Sugars:
brown sugar
granulated sugar

Frozen Goods:
petite peas
orange juice

Vegetables:
garlic
shallot
onion

Nuts & Dried Fruits:
pine nuts
roasted peanuts
Oregon hazelnuts
Oregon walnuts
slivered almonds
macadamia nuts
dried cranberries

Spices:
salt & pepper   nutmeg
cayenne pepper   onion powder
ground cumin   coriander
red pepper flakes Kosher salt
ground ginger   black peppercorns
dried oregano
dried thyme
dried dill
chili powder
paprika
Mexican chili powder
ground turmeric
bay leaf
dry mustard
dried rosemary
dried tarragon
sesame seeds
lemon pepper
Montreal seasoning

Dairy, Cheese, Refrigerator:
eggs
sour cream
butter
sharp cheddar cheese
Parmesan cheese
Feta cheese
Oregon blue cheese
Romano cheese

Canned Bottled & Packaged:
Heinz chili sauce
catsup
Tabasco sauce
Teriyaki sauce
Pesto sauce
Thai fish sauce
soy sauce
Worcestershire sauce
marinated artichoke hearts
capers
Nicoise olives
Kalamata olives
Ramen noodles-chicken flavor
Old El Paso Taco seasoning
mayonnaise
Dijon mustard
Horseradish mustard
horseradish
anchovy paste
Catalina dressing
black olives
asparagus tips
chicken stock
black beans
kidney beans
Bush's pinto beans
croutons
Nacho Cheese Doritos
flour tortilla wraps
tostada shells
honey
molasses
hickory smoked BBQ sauce
Mango chutney
Hidden Valley Ranch dressing pkt.
Chipolte chilies in adobo sauce

CONTENTS

CONTENTS

CONTENTS

CONTENTS

Crab Louis

Crab Louis

Ingredients:

◆ ½ lb. Fresh Oregon Dungeness Crabmeat

1/4 cup sour cream

1/4 cup mayonnaise

2 T. Heinz chili sauce

◆ 1/8 cup fine chopped green or red pepper

◆ 1/8 cup fine chopped green onion

◆ 1 ½ t. lemon juice

Tabasco - 6 drops or to taste

½ t. prepared horseradish

½ t. Worcestershire sauce

salt and pepper

◆ 1 small head iceberg lettuce

◆ 2 large ripe tomatoes (wedged)

2 hard cooked eggs (wedged)

Garnishes: black olives, asparagus tips, capers,
◆ parsley sprigs, ◆ lemon wedges

Direction:

In a medium bowl, combine sour cream, mayonnaise, chili sauce, bell pepper, onion, lemon juice, horseradish, and Worcestershire sauce. Season with salt, pepper, and Tabasco sauce. Cover and refrigerate.

Arrange 2 or 3 outer lettuce leaves (or radicchio leaves) on two plates. Shred remaining lettuce (about 6 cups), divide and place onto leaf lined plates. Shred all but 4 crab legs (use remaining legs for garnish) and mound onto shredded lettuce. Sprinkle with salt and pepper. Arrange tomato, egg, asparagus, olives and capers on top. Pour on ½ of dressing. Garnish with crab legs, parsley and lemon wedges. Serve remaining dressing separately.

(Note: may substitute bay shrimp for crabmeat.)

Chicken With Spicy Corn Salad

Chicken With Spicy Corn Salad

Ingredients:

- ✦ (1) Deli-roasted chicken (plain or barbecue)
- ✦ ½ small red bell pepper, diced
- ✦ 2 cups fresh corn kernels
- ✦ 1 cup fresh green beans (trimmed and sliced diagonally into ½" pieces)

1/4 cup extra virgin olive oil

- ✦ 1/3 cup fresh lime juice
- ✦ 1 T. (or to taste) green poblano chili (seeded and fine chopped)

salt & pepper, to taste

½ t. cayenne pepper

1/4 t. ground cumin

- ✦ 6 green onions (sliced diagonally)
- ✦ 1/4 cup chopped cilantro
- ✦ 3 T. fresh cilantro leaves (garnish)

Direction:

In a skillet, saute corn, green beans and red pepper in 1 T. olive oil until tender crisp. Set aside. In a large bowl, whisk together the remaining olive oil, lime juice, chili, salt & pepper to taste, cayenne pepper and cumin. Add the corn, beans, and remaining ingredients and stir to combine. Allow to rest for 2 minutes. Stir. Divide mixture onto 2 serving plates. Top salad with chicken pieces, and garnish with cilantro leaves.

Northwest Salmon Salad

Northwest Salmon Salad

Ingredients:

✦ ½ lb. fresh Northwest salmon

1 T. *each*, oil & butter

✦ 4 cups assorted greens (frisee, radicchio, arugula)

Vinaigrette:

1 T. honey

1 ½ T. Balsamic vinegar

1 t. Dijon mustard

½ shallot, minced

1/3 cup extra virgin olive oil

salt and pepper, to taste

Relish:

✦ 3 heirloom tomatoes, seeded & diced large

✦ ½ t. fresh rosemary, minced

✦ 3 basil leaves, chopped

1 t. Balsamic vinegar

1/4 cup extra virgin olive oil

Direction:

Mix together greens and refrigerate.

Boil 1 ½ T. Balsamic vinegar and 1 T. honey, and reduce by one half. Add Dijon mustard, shallot, salt and pepper. Gradually whisk in 1/3 cup olive oil. Set aside.

Mix together relish and set aside.

Pan sear salmon in oil and butter, until nicely browned and cooked. (alternately, you may brush with a little vinaigrette and grill)

Toss salad greens with one tablespoon of vinaigrette. Place on the center of plates. Place salmon on top, and surround with tomato relish.

Warm Chicken Spinach Salad

Warm Chicken Spinach Salad

Ingredients:

- ½ lb. boneless, skinless chicken breast
  (thin sliced)
- 1 T. olive oil
- 1 t. crushed garlic
- 6 mushrooms, sliced
- 2 Roma tomatoes (seeded and diced)
- 1 green onion, sliced
- 1/4 cup chicken stock
- 1 T. fresh lemon juice
- 1/4 t. red pepper flakes
- 2 cups baby spinach (stems removed)
- 2 T. toasted pine nuts
- 3 T. shaved (or grated) Parmesan cheese
- ½ lb. pasta (bow ties, fussili, or fettucine)

Direction:

Cook pasta 10 minutes, or until al dente. Drain and cool.

Heat 1 ½ t.olive oil on high heat in skillet. Saute chicken pieces 2 to 3 minutes until done. Season with salt and pepper, and set aside. Add remaining oil to pan. Add garlic, mushrooms, tomatoes, and onion and saute 1 minute. Add vegetables to reserved chicken. In the same skillet add stock, lemon juice, red pepper flakes, and bring to a boil. Add reserved chicken mixture, pasta, and toss together. Remove from heat. Toss warm pasta mixture with spinach leaves. Serve immediately, dividing onto two serving plates. Sprinkle with pine nuts and Parmesan cheese.

Marinated Pepper Steak Salad

Marinated Pepper Steak Salad

Ingredients:

+ 3 cups rare roast beef, cut into thin strips
+ 2 tomatoes, cut into wedges
+ ½ green pepper, cut into strips
+ ½ red pepper, cut into strips
+ 1 cup celery, sliced
+ 1/3 cup green onion, sliced
+ 1/3 cup fresh mushrooms, sliced
+ 4 cups mixed greens

Marinade: ½ cup teriyaki sauce
1/3 cup dry sherry
1/3 cup salad oil
3 T. white vinegar
½ t. ground ginger

<u>Direction</u>:

Combine ingredients for marinade in a jar;
shake well.

Combine beef, tomatoes, peppers, celery, onion,
and mushrooms. Toss with marinade to coat.

Cover and refrigerate 2 to 3 hours.

Drain, reserving marinade. Place greens on two
plates. Top with marinated meat and vegetables.
Pass reserved marinade for dressing.

Pesto Pasta Salad With Chicken

Pesto Pasta Salad With Chicken

<u>Ingredients:</u>

(1) 8 oz. jar of Christopher Ranch pesto

✦ (1) boneless, skinless chicken breast

✦ (1) grilled yellow or orange bell pepper

✦ (3) oven roasted plum tomatoes

1 T. olive oil

1 ½ t. dried oregano

1 ½ t. dried thyme

salt and pepper

½ cup freshly grated Romano cheese

½ lb (8 oz) farfalle or pappardelle noodles

Direction:

Preheat oven to 400 degrees. Core and stem tomatoes and slice in half lengthwise. Scoop out seeds and then cut into quarters. Place in small ovenproof dish and drizzle with oil, season with salt and pepper, oregano, and thyme. Roast 30 minutes. Cool. Coat chicken with 2 T. pesto and grill until cooked. Let rest 10 minutes, then cut into strips.

Grill pepper until evenly charred. Place in paper bag for 10 minutes, remove skin, seed and cut into thin strips. Cook pasta, drain and cool. Put pasta back into pot and drizzle with a bit of olive oil. Stir in remaining pesto. Add tomatoes, chicken, and pepper slices. Transfer to a large bowl. Sprinkle with Romano cheese, season with freshly ground pepper, and toss. Cover and refrigerate. Best served at room temperature.

Thai Chicken And Noodle Salad

Thai Chicken And Noodle Salad

Ingredients:

✦ ½ lb. boneless, skinless chicken breast (cut into
1 T. peanut oil   strips)
pinch of red pepper flakes

✦ 1/4 lb. shitake mushrooms, sliced

✦ 1/4 cup *each* carrots, snow peas, celery, red
onion (julienne)

✦ ½ cup red bell pepper, julienne

2 cups hot, cooked capellini pasta

✦ 8 butter or red lettuce leaves

✦ 2 T. chopped cilantro

1/8 cup roasted peanuts

Dressing:

1/4 cup rice wine vinegar

✦ 1 T. fresh ginger, minced   pinch of cayenne

1/4 cup honey   1 T. hot chili oil

1 T. soy sauce   1 T. sesame oil

1 t. minced garlic   2 T. salad oil

Direction:

Mix together dressing ingredients and set aside.
Heat peanut oil in skillet and add chicken and red
pepper flakes. Cook until meat is no longer pink,
and cooked. Remove from pan and set aside.

In the same skillet, add the mushrooms and onions
and cook 1 minute. Add remaining vegetables and
cook 1 minute longer.

In large bowl, combine cooked chicken, noodles,
and vegetable mixture. Add dressing and mix
thoroughly.

Line plates with lettuce leaves, top with noodle
salad mixture. Garnish with cilantro and roasted
peanuts. Can be served hot or cold.

Salmon Salad Nicoise

Salmon Salad Nicoise

<u>Ingredients</u>:

1 ½ t. Dijon mustard, 1/4 t. anchovy paste

1 clove garlic, minced

½ t. sugar

pinch of tarragon

1/8 cup white wine vinegar

salt and pepper

1/4 cup extra virgin olive oil

✦ 2 sups salad greens

✦ 3 small yellow Finn or fingerling potatoes

✦ 1/4 lb. pea pods (or green beans) blanched

✦ 2 plum tomatoes, sliced

✦ ½ small red onion, sliced in thin rings

4 artichoke hearts, cut in half

2 hard cooked eggs, quartered

½ cup nicoise olives, ✦ lemon wedges

✦ 1 ½ cups flaked, cooked Northwest Salmon

<u>Direction</u>: .

Steam, peel and slice the potatoes. Combine mustard, garlic, sugar, tarragon, vinegar, salt, pepper and anchovy paste. Slowly whisk in oil. Set aside.

Arrange greens on two plates. Add potatoes, pea pods, tomatoes, onion rings, artichoke hearts, eggs, salmon, and olives. Spoon on dressing. Garnish with lemon wedges.

Southwest Pork Tenderloin Corn Salad

Southwest Pork Tenderloin Corn Salad

Ingredients:

✦ ½ lb. pork tenderloin

3/4 t. *each* salt cumin, chili powder, black pepper

3/4 t. *each* granulated sugar and brown sugar

3/4 t. *each* onion powder, ground coriander

1 ½ t. paprika

✦ 2 cups fresh corn kernels

1 shallot, minced

1/4 cup black beans, rinsed

✦ 1 cup diced, cooked potatoes

✦ ½ red pepper, diced

1/4 cup vinegar

pinch sugar

pinch red pepper flakes

salt and pepper, to taste

2 T. olive oil

Direction:

In a small bowl, mix together rub spices (3/4 t.
salt, sugar, cumin, brown sugar, chili powder,
black pepper, onion powder, ground coriander;
paprika).   Heat oven to 425 degrees. Season
tenderloin with rub. Place tenderloin in shallow
pan and roast 30 to 35 minutes, or until internal
temperature is 170 degrees. Remove from oven
and let stand 10 minutes.

In a large skillet, saute corn and red pepper flakes
in 1 T. olive oil for 2 minutes. Mix all of
remaining ingredients together.

Divide salad and place on two plates. Slice pork
and place on top of salad.

Taco Salad

Taco Salad

Ingredients:
- ✦ ½ lb. lean ground beef
- ✦ ½ onion, chopped
- 1 cup kidney or pinto beans, rinsed and drained
- 1/4 cup Catalina dressing
- 1/4 cup water
- 1/4 cup sliced black olives
- 1 ½ t. Mexican chili powder
- ✦ 3 cups shredded lettuce
- ✦ 1/4 cup sliced green onions
- 1 cup sharp cheddar cheese, grated
- 1 cup crushed Nacho Cheese Doritos
- ✦ Lettuce leaves (to line plates)

Garnishes: sour cream
- ✦ avocado slices
- ✦ chopped tomatoes

Direction:

Brown beef and onion in skillet. Stir in beans, dressing, water, olives and chili powder. Simmer 15 minutes.

In a large bowl, toss shredded lettuce, green onion, and 3/4 cup cheese. Add meat mixture and toss lightly.

Line two plates with lettuce leaves. Divide salad mixture onto lettuce leaves. Sprinkle each with remaining 1/4 cup cheese and crushed Doritos. Add garnishes and serve.

Chicken Turmeric Rice Salad

Chicken Turmeric Rice Salad

<u>Ingredients:</u>

✦(1) Deli-roasted chicken cut into bite-sized pcs.

½ cup long grain white rice

1/8 t. ground turmeric

½ bay leaf

<u>*Dressing:*</u>　✦ ½ t. lemon zest

✦ 1 T. lemon juice

1 t. Dijon mustard

½ clove garlic, minced

3 T. olive oil

salt and pepper to taste

✦ ½ cup petite peas

✦ 1/8 cup chopped parsley

✦ 2 plum tomatoes seeded and fine chopped

✦ butter lettuce to line plates

Direction:

To make dressing: mix lemon zest, lemon juice, Dijon mustard and garlic. Whisk in oil slowly, and season with salt and pepper.

In saucepan, place rice, turmeric and bay leaf. Level rice in pan, and add enough water to measure from the top of the rice, to the first knuckle of your little finger. Bring to boil and simmer 20 minutes. Remove bay leaf. Transfer to a large bowl and mix with dressing. Add peas and parsley to mixture.

Line plates with lettuce. Mound on salad. Sprinkle with chopped tomato. Top with chicken. Best served at room temperature.

Italian Penne Artichoke Salad

Italian Penne Artichoke Salad

Ingredients:

½ lb. penne pasta or shells

✦ ½ lb. boneless, skinless chicken breast

Dressing: 1/4 cup extra virgin olive oil

✦ 1/8 cup lemon juice

1 clove garlic, minced

½ t. dried oregano

2 t. chicken stock

2 T. Parmesan cheese, grated

1/8 t. black pepper

pinch sugar

1 (6 oz.) jar marinated artichoke hearts

(reserve marinade)

✦ 1 small red pepper (seeded and sliced thin)

1/4 cup sliced black olives

✦ lettuce leaves to line plates

<u>Direction</u>:

Thinly slice the chicken breasts.
Cook pasta according to directions on package.
Rinse and drain. Mix in 1 tablespoon of olive oil.
Set aside. Mix together dressing ingredients,
whisking in oil at the last. In skillet, saute
chicken in the reserved artichoke marinade. Cool.
In a large bowl, mix pasta, chicken, artichoke
hearts, red pepper, olives and dressing. Cover
and chill. Serve on lettuce lined plates.

Chicken Apple Hazelnut Salad

Chicken Apple Hazelnut Salad

Ingredients:

✦ 5 Romaine lettuce leaves

✦ 5 red leaf lettuce leaves

✦ 1 red apple, chopped

✦ 1/3 red onion, cut into thin rings

1/4 cup Oregon filberts (hazelnuts) chopped

1/4 cup croutons

1/3 cup Parmesan cheese, grated

✦ 2 poached or grilled chicken breasts, julienne

Dressing: ✦ 1/4 cup fresh lemon juice

1 T. light rice vinegar

1/4 t. Dijon mustard

2 cloves garlic, minced

1/4 cup olive oil

2 T.Canola oil

1/4 t. fresh ground pepper

<u>Direction</u>:

Combine dressing ingredients, whisking in oils last. Set aside.

Tear lettuce into a large bowl. Add remaining ingredients except chicken. Toss with 2-3 tablespoons of dressing. Arrange greens on plates and top with chicken. Add more dressing if desired.

Note: chicken may be basted with a little dressing before cooking, if grilled or baked.

Marinated Chicken Caesar Salad

Marinated Chicken Caesar Salad

Ingredients:

✦ (2) hearts of romaine lettuce
✦ (2) boneless skinless chicken breasts
sliced artichoke hearts for garnish
1/3 cup grated Parmesan cheese

Dressing: 1 clove garlic, minced
        1/4 t. dry mustard
        1/4 t. Worcestershire sauce
        1 T. wine vinegar
        ✦ 1 T. lemon juice
        1/4 cup olive oil
        1 hard cooked egg (chop fine)
        1 T. grated Parmesan cheese
        salt and pepper to taste

Croutons: 1 clove garlic,
        1/4 c. olive oil
        1/2 cup cubed french bread

<u>Direction</u>:

Combine dressing ingredients in blender, and blend until smooth. Add salt to taste. Let stand 30 minutes at room temperature.

Baste chicken with 1 tablespoon of dressing and bake 35 to 40 minutes at 350 degrees. After baking, baste again with 1 tablespoon of dressing. Cool.

Place lettuce on plates. Top with chicken breast. Drizzle with dressing. Sprinkle with remaining Parmesan cheese and croutons (purchased, or recipe follows). Garnish with sliced artichoke hearts.

<u>*Croutons*</u>: Soak garlic in oil overnight; discard garlic. Toss bread cubes in oil and spread on baking sheet. Bake 350 degrees for 5-10 minutes, turning frequently, until lightly browned.

Warm Chicken Artichoke Pasta Salad

Warm Chicken Artichoke Pasta Salad

Ingredients:

½ lb. bow tie pasta

1 T. pine nuts

1 ½ t. olive oil

✦ ½ lb. boneless skinless chicken breasts (thin slice)

✦ 1 small red pepper (seeded and thin sliced)

1 shallot, minced

1 clove garlic, minced

½ cup chicken stock

1/8 cup Balsamic vinegar

½ t. dried rosemary

(1) 6 oz. jar marinated artichoke hearts

pinch of red pepper flakes

Parmesan cheese (shaved or grated)

Direction:

Cook pasta 10 minutes. Drain and cool. Toast pine nuts in a non-stick skillet on medium heat until golden. Set aside. Heat oil on high heat in skillet and saute chicken strips for 2 to 3 minutes until done. Season with salt and pepper, and set aside.

In the same skillet, saute peppers, shallots, and garlic for 2 minutes, until tender crisp. Add to reserved chicken. Add to skillet: stock, vinegar, rosemary and red pepper flakes. Bring to boil. Add artichokes and reserved chicken mixture to pan. Add pasta and toss just until warmed. Divide onto two plates. Sprinkle with pine nuts and Parmesan cheese. Serve warm.

Island Shrimp Salad

Island Shrimp Salad

Ingredients:

✦ 1 lb. cooked large shrimp, shelled & deveined

✦ 1 papaya, peeled, seeded and sliced

✦ 1 mango, peeled, seeded and sliced

✦ 1/4 fresh pineapple, cut into spears

✦ 1 avocado, peeled, seeded and sliced

✦ 1 kiwi fruit, sliced

✦ butter lettuce

Dressing: ✦ 1/4 cup whipping cream

1 T. grated sweetened coconut

✦ 1 T. lime juice

✦ 1 ½ t. grated lime or lemon rind

1 t. honey

✦ ½ t. grated fresh ginger

1/8 cup mayonnaise

Garnishes: toasted coconut, chopped macadamia nuts, ✦grapes and ✦mint.

<u>Direction</u>: .

Line plates with butter lettuce. Arrange shrimp in center of plate with fruit attractively placed around it.

Combine dressing ingredients, except mayonnaise, in a blender and whirl until fluffy. Fold mixture into mayonnaise. Place a dollop of dressing on each salad and accompany with toasted coconut, macadamia nuts, grapes and mint.

Note: slices of cooked chicken breast may be substituted for shrimp.

Chicken Salad Nicoise

Chicken Salad Nicoise

Ingredients:

✦ ½ lb. boneless skinless chicken breasts

1 T. olive oil

1/4 t. salt

1/8 t. pepper

✦ 1/4 t. chopped fresh rosemary

✦ ½ lb. small new potatoes

✦ 1/4 lb. green beans, trimmed, blanched 3 min.

2 hard-boiled eggs, cut into wedges

✦ 2 tomatoes, cut into wedges

1/4 cup pitted Nicoise olives

✦ 1/4 t. chopped fresh tarragon (or dried)

✦ 1/8 cup chopped fresh basil or parsley

Dressing: 1 ½ T. red wine vinegar; 1/2 t. anchovy paste; 1 garlic clove (finely chopped) 1 t. pepper, 1 t. Dijon mustard, 1/4 c. olive oil

<u>Direction</u>:

Pat chicken dry with paper towels. Stir together oil, salt, pepper, and rosemary. Place chicken in oil mixture. Marinate several hours. Grill on oiled barbecue over medium heat until cooked. Let cool and cut into strips.

Stir together dressing ingredients. Set aside. Cook potatoes; halve, chop, and drizzle with a little dressing while still warm. Divide potatoes and place in center of two plates. Surround potatoes with a ring of green beans, then eggs and tomatoes. Top potatoes with strips of grilled chicken. Sprinkle with olives, tarragon and basil. Pour salad dressing over just before serving.

Note: may add red onion rings and capers, if desired.

Greek Salad With Broiled Shrimp

Greek Salad with Broiled Shrimp

Ingredients:

✦ 8 medium shrimp

✦ 1/2 t. fresh oregano (1/4 t. dried)

2 T. olive oil

1 clove garlic, minced

salt and pepper

✦ 2 tomatoes, cut into wedges or chunks

✦ 1 Lebanese cucumber, peeled seeded & sliced

✦ ½ green pepper, sliced

✦ 1/4 red onion, finely sliced

1 T. extra virgin olive oil

½ t. red wine vinegar

8 Kalamata olives

✦ 6 fresh mint leaves, coarse chop

✦ 1 ½ T. fresh Italian parsley leaves, coarse chop

fresh ground black pepper

3 oz. Feta cheese

Direction:

Peel shrimp, leave tails on, remove veins. Place in bowl and toss with oregano, 2 T. olive oil, garlic, salt and pepper. Thread shrimp onto two metal skewers. Place on baking sheet, and broil 2 to 3 minutes (until tops are brown). Turn and cook 2 to 3 minutes more. Set aside.

Put tomatoes, cucumber, green pepper, onion, and olive oil in bowl. Toss to combine and set aside for 10 minutes. Add vinegar, olives, mint, parsley and pepper. Mix. Transfer to plates and crumble Feta cheese on top. Top with shrimp.

May line plates with lettuce, if desired.

Cobb Salad

 *Cobb Salad*

Ingredients:

✦ 4 cups mixed salad greens of choice

✦ 2 chicken breast halves, cooked and fine diced

1/3 cup Oregon blue cheese, crumbled

✦ 1 avocado, peeled and diced

6 slices bacon, cooked crisp and crumbled

2 hard cooked eggs, peeled and chopped

✦ 2 medium tomatoes, peeled and chopped

✦ 1 T. chopped chives

olives, ✦ radishes, ✦ avocado slices for garnish

Dressing: 1/4 t. dry mustard

1/4 c. red wine vinegar

✦ 1 ½ t. lemon juice

3/4 t. Worcestershire sauce

½ clove garlic, minced

1/3 cup olive oil

1/4 t. sugar, ½ t. salt, 3/4 t. pepper

Direction:

Combine dressing ingredients, whisking in oil. Set aside. Line plates with torn salad greens. Mix together salad ingredients and divide onto lettuce lined plates. (or, arrange equal portions of salad toppings in individual rows over salad greens) Pour dressing on salads. Garnish with olives, radishes, and avocado slices.

Note: smoked turkey may be substituted for chicken.

Pear Chicken Walnut Salad

Pear Chicken Walnut Salad

Ingredients:

✦ 3/4 lb. boneless, skinless chicken breasts

1 ½ cups chicken broth

Dressing: 1 ½ t. Dijon mustard

1/8 t. garlic, minced

1/8 t. shallot, minced

✦ 1 ½ t. fine chopped basil, thyme,
or tarragon

1 T. tarragon vinegar

1/4 cup mild flavored vegetable oil

✦ 1 ½ T. fresh lemon juice

1/8 t. salt and pepper

✦ 1 Asian pear, peeled and sliced

½ cup chopped walnuts

✦ 1 cup fresh spinach leaves, stems removed

✦ 1 head butter lettuce, torn

walnut halves for garnish

<u>Direction</u>: .

Cook chicken breasts in broth in a foil covered pan, at 350 degrees for 30 minutes. Cool and julienne. Combine dressing ingredients, whisking in oil. Set aside.

Combine in a large bowl: pears (reserve a few slices for garnish), spinach, lettuce, and chopped walnuts.   Add chicken. Toss with dressing. Divide mixture onto two plates. Garnish with walnut halves and a few of the pear slices.

Ramen Chicken Salad

Ramen Chicken Salad

<u>Ingredients</u>:

✦ 2 cups cooked chicken (shredded or chopped)

✦ 2 cups shredded cabbage or lettuce

1 pkg. Ramen noodles (chicken flavored)

2 T. sesame seeds

✦ 2 green onions, chopped

1/3 cup dried cranberries (optional)

✦ lettuce leaves (for lining plates)

2 oz. toasted slivered almonds

✦ melon slices, grapes, pineapple slices (optional garnishes)

<u>Dressing:</u> 1 seasoning packet (Ramen noodle pkg)

1/3 cup oil

3 T. vinegar

1 T. sugar

½ t. *each* salt and pepper

<u>Direction</u>:

Mix dressing ingredients and shake well.
In a large bowl, mix chicken, cabbage, ½ package
Ramen noodles crumbled, sesame seeds, onion,
and cranberries. Add dressing and mix. Cover
and refrigerate overnight. (Note: may serve
immediately, if crunchier noodles desired.)
Line plates with lettuce. Top with salad. Sprinkle
with almonds and remaining crumbled Ramen
noodles. Garnish and surround with melon slices,
grapes, and pineapple slices, if desired.

Tortilla Salad

 *Tortilla Salad*

Ingredients:

(2) large flour tortilla wraps

2 t. light oil

✦ 3/4 lb. lean ground beef

1 package Old El Paso Taco Seasoning Mix

1 (16 oz.) can Bush's Best pinto beans (or
        kidney beans), rinsed and drained

1 cup grated sharp cheddar cheese

✦ 1/4 head iceberg lettuce, finely shredded

1/3 cup sour cream

✦ 1 avocado

✦ 1 ripe tomato

✦ fresh lime juice

salt and pepper

black olives for garnish

<u>Direction</u>:

Preheat oven to 375 degrees. Mold the flour tortillas into flat-bottomed, ovenproof, medium sized tins or bowls. The idea is to make a bowl to contain the salad. Bake for 10-12 minutes until crisp and golden.

Heat the oil in skillet and fry beef until well browned. Add taco seasoning, ½ cup water, and bring to a boil. Add beans and simmer 8 minutes. Seed, peel and dice the avocado. Seed and dice the tomato. Combine avocado and tomato, squeeze lime juice over and season with salt and pepper.

Fill cooked shell with beef mixture, then grated cheese, and shredded lettuce. Add dollops of sour cream, and top with avocado mixture. Garnish with black olives.

Tarragon Chicken Salad

Tarragon Chicken Salad

Ingredients:

◆ 2 1/2 cups cooked chicken, shredded or chopped

◆ 1/4 lb. seedless red grapes

2 oz. toasted walnut halves

Dressing:

1/3 cup sour cream

1 T. Dijon mustard

3 T. mayonnaise

◆ 1 ½ t. chopped fresh tarragon

salt and pepper

◆ 1/4 cup chopped red onion

◆ 1/4 cup diced celery

◆ 4 oz. Brie cheese, cubed

<u>Direction</u>:

Place the chopped tarragon in a small dish or cup and add about 1 teaspoon of boiling water. Let sit for about 5 minutes. This releases the flavor of the herb. Combine the sour cream, Dijon mustard, mayonnaise, tarragon, salt and pepper.

Cut the grapes in half and combine with the chicken and toasted walnuts. Add the red onion, celery, and cheese to the chicken mixture. Fold the dressing into the chicken mixture, and chill until ready to serve. Serve with crusty bread.

Note: this makes a great sandwich as well—just halve a baguette lengthwise.

Barbecued Salmon Corn Salad

Barbecued Salmon Corn Salad

<u>Ingredients</u>:

✦ (2) 6 oz. fresh Northwest Salmon fillets

<u>Marinade:</u> ½ t. lemon pepper

　　　　　　1/8 cup vegetable oil

　　　　　　✦ 1 ½ t. lemon juice

　　　　　　1 ½ t. soy sauce

　　　　　　1/4 t. *each* dried thyme & oregano

　　　　　　1 clove garlic, minced

✦ 2 cups fresh corn kernels

1/4 cup olive oil

✦ 1 cup diced cooked Yukon gold potatoes

✦ ½ cup each, red pepper and celery, diced

✦ 1/4 cup scallions, chopped

✦ 1 T. diced Poblano (or long green) chili

1/3 cup red wine vinegar

✦ 2 T. cilantro, chopped

salt and pepper, to taste

<u>Direction</u>:

Mix ingredients for marinade.

Place salmon fillets in a glass dish and marinate for one hour. Cover the barbecue grate with two layers of heavy duty foil. Place fillets on foil, skin side down. Do not turn when cooking. Grill on medium heat for 20 to 25 minutes. When done remove meat only with a spatula, leaving skin on foil. Set aside.

In skillet, saute corn in 1 tablespoon olive oil for 2 minutes. Cool.

Mix together all salad ingredients. Divide between two plates, and top with pieces of barbecued salmon.

Grilled Lemon Chicken Salad

 Grilled Lemon Chicken Salad

Ingredients:
- ✦ 1 lb. boneless, skinless chicken breasts
- ✦ 2 cups mixed julienned peppers
    (red, yellow, orange)
- ✦ 1 cup green peas, snow peas, or sugar snap

                                        peas

- ✦ 1/3 cup thin sliced red onion

Marinade: ✦ 1/4 cup fresh lemon juice
            1/4 cup olive oil
            3/4 t. salt
            ½ t. fresh ground pepper
            1 ½ t. dried thyme
            1 ½ t. dried oregano

Dressing: 3 T. extra virgin olive oil
            1/4 t. salt
            1/4 t. fresh ground pepper

Direction:

In a small bowl, mix together marinade ingredients. Pour over chicken breasts, cover with plastic wrap and refrigerate 4 hours or overnight. Preheat grill to medium. Lightly oil grill rack. Grill chicken until marks appear and it is cooked through (about 8 minutes on each side.). Let cool 20 minutes, and slice diagonally into 1/2-inch thick slices. (chicken can be cooked a day ahead and kept covered in refrigerator).

Whisk together dressing ingredients.

In a large bowl, toss peppers, peas, onion, and grilled lemon chicken slices with the dressing.

Add additional salt and pepper if desired. Serve cold or at room temperature.

Thai Grilled Beef Salad

Thai Grilled Beef Salad

Ingredients:

✦ 1 lb. New York steak

✦ 8 oz. Arugula

✦ 6 oz. seedless red grapes, halved

1 T. toasted sesame seeds

✦ 2 stems lemongrass, tender inner part only,
sliced thin (optional)

Marinade: ✦ 3 hot red chilies (bird's eye)

✦ 2 cloves garlic, peeled

✦ 1 inch fresh ginger, peeled

✦ 2 T. *each*, chopped fresh
coriander, basil, and mint

4 T. Thai fish sauce

✦ 4 T. fresh lime juice

✦ grated zest of 1 lemon & 1 lime

2 t. brown sugar

Direction:

Combine marinade ingredients in blender and blend until smooth. Reserve.

Lightly oil grill rack and preheat to high. Grill steak for 2 to 3 minutes on each side. (the beef will appear undercooked, but the lime juice in the marinade will finish it.) Let beef rest for 10 minutes, then slice diagonally into 3/8" thick slices. Place beef slices and any juices in bowl with marinade. Cover and refrigerate 1 hour or overnight.

When ready to serve, toss beef with arugula and grapes and arrange on a platter. Use the marinade as the dressing. Sprinkle with sesame seeds and lemongrass.

Note: When you barbecue steaks for a meal, just add 1 extra steak, and make this salad the next day.

Garlic Romaine Salad

Garlic Romaine Salad

<u>Ingredients</u>:

✦ 2 hearts of Romaine lettuce, washed & crisped

✦ 1 ripe avocado, peeled and diced

3 T. grated Parmesan cheese

✦ 1 cup cherry tomatoes, halved

✦ 2 green onions, thinly sliced

2/3 cup seasoned croutons

<u>*Dressing:*</u>   ✦ 2 cloves garlic, minced

½ t. salt

✦ 1 T. lime or lemon juice

1 egg white (or 1 T. olive oil)

1/3 cup mayonnaise

2 t. Worcestershire or soy sauce

Note: may add salad topper of your choice, such as crab, shrimp, chicken, salmon. (see page 133)

<u>Direction</u>:

Combine garlic and salt, and mash into a paste.
Stir in lime juice; add egg and beat until foamy.
Stir in mayonnaise and Worcestershire sauce.
Refrigerate.

Tear lettuce into bite-sized pieces. Combine in a
salad bowl with avocado, cheese, tomatoes,
onions and croutons. Add salad dressing, toss
and serve.

Montreal Steak Salad

Montreal Steak Salad

<u>Ingredients</u>:

✦ ½ lb. New York steak
Montreal seasoning
2 t. olive oil

✦ 2 hearts of Romaine lettuce
1/3 cup grated Parmesan cheese

<u>*Dressing:*</u>   ½ t. Dijon mustard
1/8 cup Balsamic vinegar
✦ 1 shallot, chopped
✦ 1 clove garlic, chopped
1/4 cup olive oil
½ t. pepper
salt

<u>Direction</u>:

Rub steak with oil, and season with Montreal seasoning. Grill 4 minutes on each side, or until desired doneness. Set aside.

Mix mustard, vinegar, shallot, and garlic in a bowl. Slowly whisk in oil. Add salt and pepper to taste. Tear romaine leaves in a large bowl. Add dressing and toss well. Divide onto plates. Sprinkle with Parmesan cheese and croutons. Slice steak thin and arrange on top.

<u>*Optional*</u> : drizzle steak with Mustard Cream

Mix together: 1 ½ t. Dijon mustard

           1/4 cup sour cream

           1/2 t. lemon juice

           salt & pepper

Seafood Tostadas

Seafood Tostadas

Ingredients:

✦ ½ lb. cooked seafood (halibut, shrimp, shark
2 Tostada shells   salmon, swordfish, crab)
½ head shredded lettuce
✦ 1/4 bunch cilantro
✦ ½ cup cucumber, chopped
✦ ½ cup bell pepper, chopped (red, yellow)
3/4 cup cooked white rice (mix with 1/4 t. salt,
                    pepper, ✦ juice of ½ lime)

Garnishes: ✦ lime wedges, guacamole, black
olives, low fat sour cream or yogurt

Guacamole: ✦ 1 ripe avocado, ✦ 1 diced tomato,
✦ 1/4 cup fine chopped red onion, ✦ ½ clove
minced garlic, ✦ 1 minced jalapeno, 1/4 t. cumin,
1/4 t. oregano, ✦ juice of 1 lime, salt & pepper

<u>Direction</u>:

For guacamole, mix all ingredients. Salt and pepper to taste. Chill.

On each plate, place a tostada shell. Spread rice on shells.

Layer fish, vegetables, lettuce, and cilantro.

Garnish as desired with lime wedges, guacamole, black olives, sour cream or yogurt.

Orecchiette Spinach Salad

Orecchiette Spinach Salad

<u>Ingredients</u>:

½ lb. orecchiette pasta (or shells)

1 t. olive oil

1 clove garlic, minced

✦ 5 oz. ricotta cheese

pinch of red pepper flakes

½ cup chicken stock

✦ ½ cup petite peas (or artichoke hearts coarse chopped)

✦ 3 oz. baby spinach (stems removed)

✦ 1 T. fresh, shredded basil leaves

✦ 6 oz. package grilled chicken breast strips
(cut into bite size pieces)

salt and pepper to taste

Parmesan cheese

✦ lemon wedges

<u>Direction</u>:

Cook pasta as directed on package. Drain, mix with a little olive oil, and keep warm.

Heat oil in a large skillet. Add garlic and cook until golden. Add ricotta, chicken stock, peas, red pepper flakes, and cook until smooth and peas are cooked. Add chicken, pasta, spinach, basil, salt and pepper to taste, and toss just until spinach begins to wilt. Transfer to plates and sprinkle generously with Parmesan cheese. Serve with lemon wedges, and crusty bread.

Northwest Indulgence
For Special Occasions

Oregon Blueberry Walnut Cobbler

½ cup sugar
1 T. cornstarch
4 cups Oregon blueberries
2 T. water
1 cup bisquick
1/4 cup milk
1/4 cup Oregon walnuts
1 T. sugar
1 T. butter, melted

Mix sugar and cornstarch in saucepan; stir in berries and water. Boil and stir 1 min. Pour into 1 ½ qt. baking dish. Stir remaining ingredients to a soft dough. Drop by tablespoon full onto hot filling. Bake at 425 degrees-15 min.

Oregon Berry Rhubarb Pie

2 ½ cups rhubarb (½" slices)
1 cup Oregon raspberries
1 cup Oregon blackberries
3/4 cup sugar
3 T. flour
1/4 t. nutmeg
dash salt
2 T. butter
1 pkg. refrigerated pie crust

Follow package directions for pie crust. Keep cold. Combine all ingredients except butter and place in dough lined 9" pie plate. Dot with cold butter. Cover with top crust and seal. Cut slits in top; brush with beaten egg; sprinkle with little sugar. Bake 400 degrees - 45 to 60 min.

Salad Toppers

Create your own version of a Main Course Salad by using your favorite salad ingredients, (or use the Garlic Romaine Salad on page 117) ,and top with any of the following recipes.

Mustard Chicken

4 boneless chicken breasts
1 t. salt
1/4 c. horseradish mustard
1 T. vinegar
2 T. water
½ t. dried thyme
1/8 t. ginger

Coat chicken with mustard mixture. Place chicken in a sprayed baking pan. Bake 30 minutes, or until done.

Barbecued Pork

1 to 2 lb. pork tenderloin
½ cup soy sauce
2 T. sugar
½ cup molasses
1/4 cup catsup
1 clove garlic, minced
½ t. MSG (optional)
2 T. honey
10 drops of red food coloring

Mix together all ingredients except pork. Place pork and sauce in ziplock and marinate 24 to 48 hours. Bake at 350 degrees for 1 ½ hours, basting every 15 minutes.

Orange Dijon Chicken

4 boneless chicken breasts
1 pkg. Hidden Valley Ranch
    dressing mix
½ cup water
1/3 c. frozen orange juice
    concentrate, thawed
2 T. Dijon mustard

Mix dressing mix, water, orange juice, and mustard. Marinate chicken for 1 hour, then bake or grill.

Mango Barbecued Prawns

6 large prawns, cooked peeled
        and deveined
1/4 cup mango chutney
1/4 cup orange juice
1/4 cup barbecue sauce
    (store bought)

Mix together chutney, orange juice and barbecue sauce. Brush prawns with sauce. Grill until opaque and cooked. Glaze with some extra sauce as they come off the grill.

Grilled Balsamic Mustard Chicken

3 boneless chicken breasts
3 T. balsamic vinegar
1 clove garlic
1 T. dried basil
1 T. honey
½ t. salt
½ t. fresh ground black pepper
½ t. dried oregano
3 T. canola oil

In blender, mix all ingredients except oil and chicken. Slowly add the oil while blender is running. Pour over chicken and marinate 1 to 3 hours. Grill 5 to 7 minutes on each side until done.

Lemon Grilled Salmon

1 lb. Northwest Salmon fillets
1 T. lemon juice
1 T. olive oil
1 ½ t. butter
1 ½ t. Dijon mustard
2 minced garlic cloves
dash of cayenne and salt
½ t. *each*, dried basil and dill
2 t. capers

Mix together in saucepan all ingredients except salmon. Simmer 5 minutes. On double thickness of foil with edges turned up, place fish skin side down. Place on grill, pour on sauce, and cover with lid. Grill 12 min. or until done.

Pepper Grilled Ahi Tuna

(2) 6 oz. Ahi tuna steaks
(1 1/4" thick)
1 T. Kosher salt
2 ½ T. coarsely crushed
black peppercorns
vegetable oil for grill
black olive tapenade

Mix salt and pepper and spread on a plate. Press tuna steaks into mixture and heavily coat all sides. Brush hot grill with oil and place steaks directly over hot fire. Cover grill and cook 2 minutes per side, or until desired doneness. Top with tapenade.

Chipolte Pork Tenderloin

2 lbs. pork tenderloin
½ cup hickory smoked barbecue
sauce
2 chipolte chiles packed in adobo
sauce, minced
2 T. olive oil
1 clove garlic, minced

Mix all ingredients in a ziplock bag and marinate 2 hours. Prepare grill to medium hot. Grill pork 9 minutes per side (or 150 degrees) basting frequently.

Caring For Salad Greens:

1. Prepare the greens (as soon as you bring them home) by carefully removing each leaf from the head of lettuce. Remove and discard any bruised or wilted leaves.

2. Submerge them in a sink full of cold water. Gently swish them around in the sink to loosen any dirt. Let sit in the water from 5 to 15 minutes.

3. Remove each leaf from the water, then vigorously shake the leaves, but do not dry them. (Note: if using immediately, pat the leaves dry in a paper towel, or use a salad spinner**)

4. In a food grade clear plastic box with lid (11" x 16" x 6" Rubbermaid) arrange leaves loosely. Cover and refrigerate. If desired, you may line the box with paper towels.

**Arugula, spinach and watercress bruise easily and are too fragile for a salad spinner. Hardier leaves such an endive, radicchio and oakleaf can be put into a salad spinner for drying.

How To Reduce A Recipe:

1. Use exactly one-half the amount of each ingredient.

2. If the divided recipe calls for less than one egg, beat up a whole egg. Measure with a tablespoon and divide.

3. Baking pans used for half recipes of cakes, pies, etc. should measure approximately half the area of those for the full recipe. Approximate baking times and oven temperatures are the same.

Measure Equivalents

Fluids:

cup	fluid oz	tbsp.	tsp	milliliter
1 (½ pint)	8 oz.	16 tbsp.	48 tsp.	237 ml
3/4	6 oz.	12 tbsp.	36 tsp.	177 ml
2/3	5 oz.	11 tbsp.	32 tsp.	158 ml
1/2	4 oz.	8 tbsp.	24 tsp.	118 ml
1/3	3 oz.	5 tbsp.	16 tsp.	79 ml
1/4	2 oz.	4 tbsp.	12 tsp.	59 ml
1/8	1 oz.	2 tbsp.	6 tsp.	30 ml
1/16	.5 oz.	1 tbsp.	3 tsp.	15 ml

2 cups = 1 pint   = 16 oz. = 473 ml
4 cups = 1 quart = 32 oz. = 946 ml
4 quarts = 1 gallon = 128 oz. = 3.784 liters

Dry:

3 tsp.	1 tbsp.	½ oz.	14.2	grams
2 tbsp.	1/8 cup	1 oz.	28.35	grams
4 tbsp.	1/4 cup	2 oz.	56.7	grams
5 1/3 tbsp.	1/3 cup	2 2/3 oz.	75.6	grams
8 tbsp.	½ cup	4 oz.	113.4	grams
12 tbsp.	3/4 cup	6 oz.	170	grams
16 tbsp.	1 cup	8 oz.	226.8	grams (½ lb)
32 tbsp.	2 cups	16 oz.	453.6	grams (1 lb)
64 tbsp.	4 cups	32 oz.	907	grams (2 lbs)

Substitutions For Emergencies

1 tbsp cornstarch (for thickening)	2 tbsp flour
1 whole egg (in cookies,etc)	2 egg yolks + 1 tbsp water
1 whole egg (in custards)	2 egg yolks
1 cup milk	½ cup evaporated milk + 1 cup water
	1/3 cup powdered milk stirred into 1 cup water
	1 cup buttermilk + ½ tsp soda
1 cup buttermilk	1 tbsp cider vinegar or lemon juice + enough milk
	to make 1 cup
1 cup sour milk	1 cup plain yogurt or 1 cup evaporated milk + 1
	tbsp vinegar
1 cup half and half	1 cup evaporated milk
1 square unsweetened chocolate (1 oz)	3 tbsp cocoa + 1 tbsp melted butter
1 cup honey	1 1/4 cup sugar + 1/4 cup liquid
1 cup canned tomatoes	1 1/3 cups chopped, peeled fresh tomatoes
	simmer 10 minutes
1 can (1 lb) tomatoes	2 1/2 cups chopped peeled fresh tomatoes
	simmer 10 minutes
1 cup cake flour	1 cup all purpose flour minus 2 tbsp
1 tsp baking powder	1/4 tsp baking soda + ½ tsp cream of tartar
1 envelope active dry yeast	1 compressed yeast cake, crumbled
1 cup corn syrup	1 cup granulated sugar + 1/4 cup liquid
	(Use liquid called for in recipe)
juice of 1 lemon	2 tbsp bottled lemon juice
1 tsp grated fresh lemon peel or zest of 1 lemon	1 tsp dry lemon peel (purchased)
juice of 1 medium orange	1/4 cup reconstituted frozen orange juice
1 cup regular strength chicken or beef broth	1 chicken or beef bouillon cube + 1 cup hot water
1 cup catsup or tomato based chili sauce	1 can (8oz) tomato sauce + ½ cup sugar and
	2 tbsp white vinegar
1 tsp dry mustard	1 tbsp prepared mustard
1/4 cup minced fresh onion	1 tbsp instant minced onion (let stand in liquid
	as directed)
1 clove garlic	1/8 tsp garlic powder
2 tbsp minced fresh parsley	1 tbsp dehydrated parsley flakes
½ tsp grated fresh ginger	1/4 tsp ground ginger
2 anchovy fillets	½ tsp anchovy paste

Weights And Measures Conversion

Ingredient	Weight	Measure
butter or shortening	1 lb	2 cups
cheese	4 oz	1 cup shredded
cottage cheese	1 lb	2 cups
cream cheese	3 oz pkg	6 tbsp
	8 oz pkg	1 cup
chocolate chips	6 oz pkg	1 cup
unsweetened chocolate	8 oz	8 squares
coconut (shredded or flaked)	4 oz	1 1/3 cups
coffee, ground	1 lb	80 tbsp
coffee, unground	1 lb	2 ½ cups
whipping cream	½ pint	1 cup (2 c. whipped)
sour cream	8 oz	1 cup
flour	1 lb	3 ½ cups (4 sifted)
	1 oz	2 tbsp
lemon juice	1 medium	2-3 tbsp
marshmallows	1 large	10 miniature
	11 lg or 110 small	1 cup
almonds	1 lb	1 3/4 cup
pecans	1 lb	2 1/4 cup
peanuts	1 lb	2 1/4 cup
walnuts	1 lb	1 2/3 cup
orange juice	1 medium	1/3 to ½ cup
brown sugar	1 lb	2 1/4 cups, packed
confectioners sugar	1 lb	3 ½ to 4 cups
granulated sugar	1 lb	2 1/4 cups
anchovies	2 fillets	½ tsp anchovy paste
gelatin	1/4 oz	3/4 tbsp (1 envelope)
dry yeast	1/4 oz	1 envelope
fresh bread crumbs	2 oz	1 cup
dry bread crumbs	1 lb	4 cups
Parmesan cheese, grated	4 oz	1 cup
mixed nuts, chopped	5 oz	1 cup
seedless raisins	5 3/4 oz	1 cup
lentils, split peas, dried beans	1 lb	2 cups
rice	1 lb	2 1/4 to 2 ½ cups

Shopping for Two

Amounts Shown For Two Servings:

FISH

whole	=	1 ½ to 2 lbs
fillets	=	3/4 lb
steaks	=	1 lb.
lobster tails	=	(2) 6 oz tails
oysters	=	1 pint
shrimp	=	1 lb.

BEEF

pot roast	=	2 lb
roast	=	3 lb
steak	=	2/3-1 lb
liver	=	½ lb
ground beef	=	½-1 lb
tenderloin	=	1 lb

CHICKEN

boneless	=	3/4-1 lb
frying	=	1 ½ lb
roasting	=	2 ½-3 ½ lb
turkey	=	4-6 lb

PORK

roast	=	3-4 lb
spareribs	=	2 lb
ham	=	1 lb.
chops	=	1-1/2 lb

VEGETABLES

artichokes	=	2 each	onions	=	1/4 -1/2 lb
asparagus	=	1 lb	peas	=	1 lb
beans	=	½ to 3/4 lbs	potatoes	=	3/4 -1lb
beets	=	1 lb	spinach	=	1 lb
broccoli	=	3/4 to 1 lb	squash	=	1 lb
cabbage	=	½ lb	tomatoes	=	1 each
carrots	=	½ lb	greens	=	1 lb.
cauliflower	=	½ sm.head	cucumber	=	1 each
celery	=	1 sm.bunch	corn	=	4 ears

Order Form

Menus From The Pacific Northwest
P.O. Box 6603
Bend, Oregon 97708
website: www.menusfromthepacificnw.com
 Note: you may order online at this website

Name _____

Address _____

City _____

State _____ Zip Code _____

Please send _____ copies of *Main Course Salads For Two From The Pacific Northwest*

Please send _____ copies of *Menus From The Pacific Northwest Volume 1*

Please send _____ copies of *Menus From The Pacific Northwest Volume 2*

Please send _____ copies of *Lite Pacific Northwest Recipes*

at $19.95 per copy plus $4.00 per copy to cover postage and handling within the U.S.A. Please make check or money order payable to: Menus From The Pacific Northwest

☐ VISA
☐ MASTERCARD   Card Number _____

 Signature _____ Expiration Date _____